# ALWAYS HAUNTED

### hallowe'en poems

*Original Illustrations*

# Other Books by
# LindaAnn LoSchiavo

A Route Obscure and Lonely [Elgin Award winner]

Concupiscent Consumption

Women Who Were Warned

Messengers of the Macabre: Hallowe'en Poems

Vampire Ventures

Apprenticed to the Night

Felones de Se: Poems about Suicide

# Advance Acclaim

**"Always Haunted"** offers us muses, enchants us with trance, and delivers haunting, bewitching poems brimming with body, movement, and spirit romance. I was left spellbound page after page!

> — Fiona Chew-Mcleod, Poetry Editor,
> Granfalloon: Speculative Fiction Zine (Canada)

This collection is a delight to every devotee of weird poetry and the weird in general. LindaAnn LoSchiavo draws upon the deep heritage of strangeness symbolized in the ancient festivals of Samhain and Hallowe'en, not to mention prior literary works ranging from Shakespeare to Washington Irving and even Emily Post. But this book is no exercise in antiquarianism: the author captures the essence of fear and presents it to a contemporary audience in well-crafted poems and prose poems, and the total of her efforts is a potent poetic gem that deserves repeated re-readings.

> — S. T. Joshi, E.I.C., Spectral Realms (USA)

A bewitching collection of poetry that feels both elemental and fantastically well-crafted. LoSchiavo has an incredible eye for the macabre that is to be found all around us.

> — Krishan Coupland, E.I.C.,
> Neon Books (Great Britain)

Necromancer LindaAnn LoSchiavo is a mystical maverick of paranormal poetry, a voice that knows how to enter the dark and find music in it.

> — Mark Benecke, President,
> Transylvanian Society of Dracula (Germany)

It's rare to find a book that can entertain, send chills down your spine, and be so informative that you are inspired to look up more about the subject. In "**Always Haunted**," LindaAnn LoSchiavo does just that. Ghosts, witches, and victims — women whose voices were silenced by circumstances — speak loudly and clearly through LoSchiavo's poetry. Their stories are at times tragic, empowering, and vengeful, as diverse as their histories, and they all return to "life" in LoSchiavo's book. She even imagines how Dracula could thrive in our world of social media. "**Always Haunted**" is definitely worth reading. Just make sure the lights are on.

    —Linda Gould, E.I.C.,

        White Enso, Author of The Diamond Tree, Japanese

        Ghost Stories and Kaidankai (Japan)

# ALWAYS HAUNTED

## hallowe'en poems

*Original Illustrations*

by

LindaAnn LoSchiavo

*Wild Ink Publishing*

A Wild Ink Publishing Publishing Original
wild-ink-publishing.com

Copyright © 2024 LindaAnn LoSchiavo
Edited by Brittany McMunn
Illustrations: Erin Caldwell
Cover: Ekaterina Orlovskaya
Author portrait: Ekaterina Orlovskaya
Layout: Abigail Wild

ISBN:  978-1-958531-73-0 (paperback)
        978-1-958531-74-7 (ebook)

To the Archduke

# Table of Contents

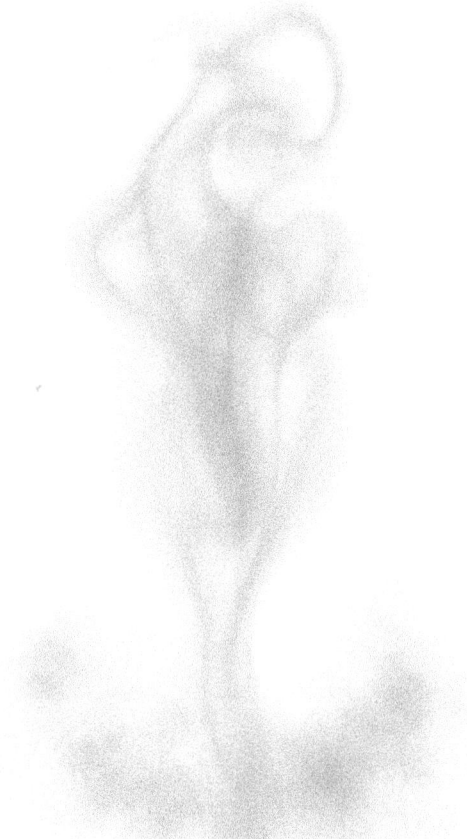

# Samhain

# Samhain

I've fallen through a rip in time tonight.

Pale outcasts perch nearby, bones tinkling,
Earth shaking with its greener mirth.  Stones creak,
Horned owls shriek as spirits gather loose clouds,
Push these exotic feather-weighted shapes
Aside — transparent curtains of their realm.

What's on the other side?  Cold hands caress
My arms invisibly.  My candle glow
Reveals no beings with a shadow.  Yet
I'm not alone, detect sweet fragrances,
Lush nectar of forbidden grapes above.
A cricket orchestra replays nocturnes.

I flutter like a trapped bird, then something
Or someone draws me in with secret steps.
A brittle leaf is plucked from my red hair.

Glass-blown interiors invite me there,
Strange iridescent skies pontilled with stars.

# A Sleepy Hollow Hallowe'en
## Inspired by Washington Irving's "The Legend of Sleepy Hollow"

Clashes with spectral hussars oft retold
By superstitious idlers keep doors locked
In Sleepy Hollow after suppertime.

October's harvest beckons thieves. We prowl
Lush farms, wheelbarrows hidden in the woods.

A jack-o-lantern moon illuminates
Gold grinning gourds, arousing appetites.

Ideal for tasty pies or windowsills,
Pumpkins pump cash into our patched pockets.

If thefts are noticed, we'd blame that horse-ghost —
Or Raven Rock's forlorn white-gowned vexed wraith,
Who haunts the dark glen where she froze to death.

Our local drunkards keep wild myths alive,
Explaining how a Hessian warrior,
Who fought alongside Brits, caught cannonfire.
Entombed without his skull, this German ghoul
Continues searching, mounted on his steed.

"Believe your eyes and ears," my father said,
"Instead of old wives' tales. Dead men lie still."

Yet I confess I'd hesitate to be
Alone within view of such restless graves —
Especially tonight, All Hallows' Eve.

With loaded sacks of fresh-picked plundered gourds,
We make our way to where we hid the cart,
Aware of hidden eyes observing us.

Fruit bats screech, scything mournful autumn skies.

Shushed evergreens' tips whisper "witching hour."
Deserted greensward. We're defenseless here.
Treetops are rustling spectral rapture: hooves.

Our brains jump their calm borders, go insane.
Damp forest floor seeps wet death through our bones.

A galloping gigantic man appears,
Wrapped in a cloak and military wear.
His head's on the protruding saddle horn.

We three disperse as fright ignites my speed.
A distant silhouette of homes greets me.

Tomorrow I'll discover my friends' fate.

Removing muddy boots, I'm now aware
This unnatural creature's real enough.

# Dracula Plans His Hallowe'en Soiree

Near Hallowe'en, routine tension sets in.

Expected entertainment, catering,
Décor: a bachelor like Dracula
Tries to outdo last year's event — though some
Attended by mistake and won't return.

Tradition dictates hospitality's
Essential to his kind.  Longevity
Must be preserved.  Drinks are but one concern.
His entourage deserves to be amused.

Instead of necks turned red as after-birth,
Refreshments can be served by a blood bank,
Thanks to a generous donation made.

Exquisite concentration on details
Is a tourniquet for his unquiet mind,
Obsessed with real estate, castle upkeep,
Demands imposed by vamphood's life-in-death.

His party plans completed, its checklist ticked,
The Transylvanian lord licked his lips,
Succumbed to tempting pleasure-crested pricks.

# Hallowe'en Horror, October 31, 2005

Calamity came calling him again,
Devised the script, cast him as "Mister Nigh,"
Quiet defiance smirking on his face as Nigh
Unzipped his skin and seized control. Dark plans
Were hatched.  October 31st.  Costumed.
His mark: a woman whom he vaguely knows.

Nigh took the wheel, refused to hear protests.
Insane schemes — toxic oxygen he breathed.

The New York cityscape burned memories
Imperfectly, erasing blue details.

Bold headlines snitched on him, his photo front
Page news. A stranger recognized his face.

Observed by aliens, Nigh disappeared,
Left Peter handcuffed and in custody.

Shackled now, he recalls he tied her up.

She testifies about her thirteen-hour
Ordeal: explosives causing smoke, enough
To fool her into opening her door,
Believing Peter was a fireman sent
To help — until he roughly ripped her clothes.

Nigh holds him captive now, detained behind
Bars, unremorseful, richly ridiculed
For blaming an accomplice never seen.

\*\*\*

Note: For his crimes on October 31, 2005, former journalist Peter
Braunstein is serving his 18-year-to-life sentence at Five Points Cor-
rectional Facility in Romulus, NY.

# Bewitchment

# Bell, Book, and Candle

I warned her, "Gillian, leave him alone.
Bewitching men is fun but keep control."

She didn't listen. Fell in love and broke
Our rules. Abandoned her familiar, too.

All Hallows' Eve the harvest moon shone red.
We chirred dark songs for her with rattling bones,
Ignited ceremonial henbane,
Amassed charged graveyard water. Then, by stealth,
We slipped inside his home, snuffed his candle.
Sweet incense of annihilation rose.

Perhaps he magicked *her* more than she him?
Infatuation is unknowable.
Emotions lack strategic wherewithal.

The coven must protect frail kith and kin
Who can't envisage misadventure's cure.

# Hetty Green, the "Witch of Wall Street"

Since Hetty Green amassed a fortune, witch
Became her nickname — mocking her acclaim.
Wall Street successes counted men not dames.
Her black coat tented over dresses stitched
To last, avoiding willful beauty, which
Retained more income. Hetty saw no shame
In practicality nor thrift, maintained
Her stringent lifestyle, growing very rich.

Her ghost embraced the witch identity,
Began to hex male enemies. What fun
To exercise her powers, cause the crash
Of 1929, wreak misery,
Observe as ill-gotten gains came undone.
It's said that her last breath was used to laugh.

\*\*\*

Note: Hetty Green [November 21, 1834 — July 3, 1916] was America's first female tycoon. At the time of her death at age 81, Hetty Green's personal fortune was estimated at $100 million and her estate rivaled those of other financiers and capitalists of the day. However, history books often portray her unfairly, describing Green only as a miser and an eccentric.

Note: The Wall Street Crash occurred on October 28, 1929.

# Secrets of the Spell

## I. Wasted Breath

Spite stirred in guts like poison mixed in cake.
Insistent maleness and disparity
Assembled heated breath, enough to hex
A British play. Heed this — or rue the day.

Old Scottish combat zones, intent on war's
Mythology and trophies, replicate
Themselves wherever men fish for acclaim
To get their stories splashed across the stars —
In letters, law, or laboratories.

When males engage with chemicals, rank brines,
Intent on alchemy, employing fire,
Rapt by discoveries perhaps benign,
They're being scientific, praised. They'll bask
In backlit glows that manly fame bestows.

       The patriarchy does its best to hoard
       Awards — like weapons needed for attacks.

When females huddle over cauldron smoke,
Ancestral recipes astir once more,
Rapt by solutions stronger than strychnine,
Which sheriff thought, *"Girls having fun outdoors!"* ?
Suspicious scribes malign spell-casting crones,
Implying they are doing devil's work.

       The patriarchy does its best to warn,
       Forbid, discourage daughters, sisters, wives
       By commandeering rights to accolades.

Distrust of women's power led to laws.
In 1542, King Henry VIII
Signed Britain's first Witchcraft Act. Hundreds died,
Even if those accused denied the charge.

## II. *Macbeth*

Elizabethan dramatists — all men! —
Put witches in the plot for novelty.
Meanwhile, witch hunts harassed the innocent.

>Misogyny's increase deserved byplay.
>Real sorceresses jinxed "the Scottish play,"
>Their hex comeuppance. Bloodshed was repaid.

*Macbeth* depicts a pagan coven — though
Their wisdom's minimized by childish speech
Like "Double, double, toil, and trouble" — rhymes
For children, to infantilize this spell.

With "eye of newt, toe of frog," thespians
Portraying the Weird Sisters cursed the Thane
Of Cawdor, who rebelled against his king.

*Macbeth*'s debut was struck — streaked with bad luck.

## III. Met Death

Before Scene 5, the Bard went backstage — found
Lady Macbeth mystifyingly dead,
Unnerving King James in his royal box.

Which elements affected Brits the most?
Staged sorcery incited constant fear
His majesty intensified with trials.

Mark my words: women have always fought back,
Preserved infernal mysteries. Bewitched.
Dark invocations learned by stealth live on.

*Macbeth*'s unholy spell won't be withdrawn
'Til every "witch's" unfair death is mourned.

\*\*\*

Note: The Scottish Play. The Bard's Play. *Macbeth* is surrounded by superstition and fear of the "curse" – that uttering the play's name aloud in a theatre will cause bad luck.

# Spellcasting on Samhain

"Night-dyed herbs," came the vendor's cry. "Come buy!
Seductive power. Risk-free trial! Please try
My wares on Samhain!" Odd plants caught my eye.

What did I have to lose? "Can you reverse
Ill-omened destiny?" The crone was terse.
"I'll handle all requests. But pay me first."

Showing your photo only made her nod,
Suspending my belief in priests, saints, God.
Entrusted with my prayers, their grace was flawed.

Counting my money like a cold cashier,
The witch's countenance conveyed a sneer.
October's dying heat lured magic near.

Stroking strange herbs with calloused palms, her quotes
Were incantations. Still inchoate, motes
Re-formed as *you* — grime hanging on your coat,

Death's tight grip meeting life's warm open hand
As you restaked your claim, breathed air once banned,
Embraced me tightly. Was this wonderland?

The crone removed herself, deft as a fawn.
Dismayed, when I looked back, you, too, were gone.

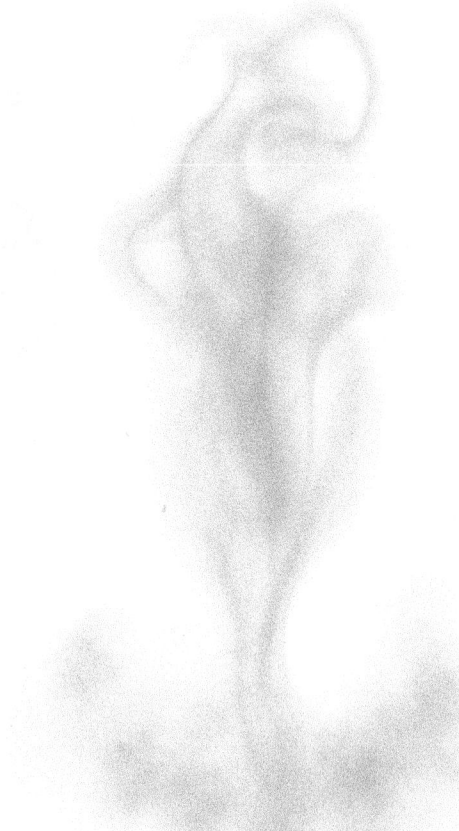

# Graveyard

# Night on Bald Mountain, All Hallows' Eve

Under a waning gibbous moon, late Fall
On All Hallows' Eve, unholy rituals
Take place as nightjars fall to their black feasts.

Old anchorites leave leafy caves, carve canes
From cypress knees, observing, their hunchbacked
Shadows distorting the infernal shapes
Twelve devotees created. Pentagrams
Appeared in the cemetery, midway
Between new monuments and older stones.

Robed figures holding torches silently
Walk widdershins, their circular footpaths
Becoming three concentric circles marked
By powder that's combustible — and now
These rings of fire leap up, light the night.

Mysteriously, as the supplicants
Position offerings inside the star,
Some tombs quake open. Skeletons emerge.

The hermits' canes, donated to the blaze,
Refuel it. Beings formed from molecules
Are welcomed as the spirits of misrule.

Nude revelers hail newborn deities.

\*\*\*

Note: Inspired by the tone poem (or musical picture) Mussorgsky
composed about St. John's Eve on Bald Mountain on the theme
of a witches' sabbath, written in 1867.

# Elizabeth Siddal Rossetti, Cemetery Superstar

Retaining fame 160 years
After I died u*nknown* — artwork unsold,
My verses unpublished — has been bizarre.

Do stars need darkness to appreciate
Their glowing? Or wise men to point them out?

My temperamental husband, mad with guilt,
Laid me to rest with poems, his bound book.
This he missed — more than my companionship.

Where's *my* work now? Just then there came a crash.

Rude crowbars pried apart my long-sealed lid.
Men open-mouthed like choristers stared shocked.

Distraught, he'd sent them. *Dig her up!* He'll learn
My flesh looked pale, my red hair's grown more wild.

Rossetti's poems sweetened maggots' meals.
Worm-eaten scraps had crowned my coffined head,
A spectral tapestry akin to my
Ophelia pose, a dead girl prettified,
Myself a teen when painted by Millais.

A painting's fame forgets dead models — but
Art helps us dream back everything that's lost.

*** 

Note: Elizabeth Siddal [1829 — 1862] wed Dante Gabriel Rossetti in 1849. In 1869, her husband's agent Charles Augustus Howell encouraged Rossetti to put an exhumation in motion to retrieve the poems from her grave.

# Erasure at Nightfall

Stealth is my friend once again. Unnoticed at lock-up time, I'm lingering among crosses set in even rows. The gridlock of grim. Typical visitor hours are too hectic, rife with bald human moments — slumping shoulders mantled in misery. All the ways bereavement can scaffold joy. A boneyard devoid of human sounds is preferable. Aware of the final, fading pulses of light, I apostrophe myself into the dark and begin. Crunching frost-crisped leaves underfoot produces a dry crackle like ghosts coughing. I approach one particular monument arrayed in its upright finery of euphemisms, letters loud with an insistence to be, unscrew a clear solution, and begin my work. Decomposing, I become contradiction's champion. Shedding an edge of slate, erasing a name, obliterating the expected encomiums. Erasure pounces as acid withers the words a line at a time, returning the stone to its gall of quiet lovelessness. In life, he quietly murdered his first wife, dropped my sister's corpse from his private plane like earth's least precious stone, then kept his crimes buried by decorating his life with diplomas and philanthropy. Her remains were never found, never graced a morgue slab nor satin-lined coffin. But tonight, on All Hallows' Eve, I feel her spirit humming, numinous as a melody from warped violins.

> cemetery duty
> stiffness in my knees
> dissipating fog

# The Hallowe'en Homicides on October 31, 1981

The crime's forgotten now — except by them.

Interred apart, in graveyards miles away,
They'll rise tonight, October 31st,
To rendezvous in Chelsea, though unseen,
Avoiding doorbells dead ahead — ringing
Assumed to be young trick or treaters not
Gunmen with handcuffs. Even the dark heaved.

Morticians plied cosmetics to disguise
Her ravaged face, a mask Liz kept in place
For their reunion's kiss-fest, lips unused
To parting in delight except for him.

Unlike romantics still alive, spirits
Don't age. Forever 20, Liz shakes free
A brunette waterfall, burrows into
Remorseful Ronald, 39, as if
Love might reverse injustice or despair.

The crime's remained unsolved for more years than
Her lifetime. Nothing new to talk about,
Old topics serve — her choice for grad school, his
Photography exhibits — anything
But shrinking their own hearts into silence,
Adrift in night's black gulf, surrounded by
Costumed ghosts, fake villains, witches masked.

October's dying heat releases the scent
Of souls it's swallowed. Drinking phantom wine,
Canoodling, they enjoy sweet brevities —
Excluded from the bridal carry, joys
Of familyhood, retirement's applause —

Both destined to be destination-less,
Blind shot like pinballs, purely at the whim
Of outside forces, 22nd Street
Drawing them back by some magnetic force
Residing in its lineage of blood.

When crows screech, cutting through pink dawn like knives,
They separate, resume eternal rest,
Its polar loneliness — 'til next Samhain.

\*\*\*

Note: On Saturday, October 31, 1981, photographer Ronald Sisman [February 19, 1942 — October 31, 1981] and his college student girlfriend Elizabeth Platzman [August 4, 1961 — October 31, 1981] were brutally bludgeoned and shot execution style in his duplex on West 22nd Street in Manhattan's Chelsea neighborhood. This crime remains unsolved.

# Day of the
# Dead

# Our Lady of the Holy Death:
# Nuestra Señora de la Santa Muerte

Maybe in this version you're a black-winged grackle, *Quiscalus mexicanus*, and I built your shrine in the air. Maybe you've become bi-lingual. Maybe you need an entourage, since your believers are doubling in number and tripling in diversity. It's hard to worship a folkloric figure from Mexico, who always feels "socially distanced," but I can arrange access to an Airbnb in East Harlem, refuge of hundreds of your *compatriotas*. Thanks to Doña Queta, devotional pioneer, safely spirited away from lung cancer, I'm raring to establish a stateside tchotchke shop, *una tienda de chucherías*, to hawk Holy Death *memento mori*: inky votive candles, Bony Lady figurines, toothsome chocolate skulls for your feast days. For you, I vow to sling borderlands Spanish slang. I'll disport myself clad in a rebozo, a huipil, or a traditional gala Tehuana dress during balls and *quinceañeras*. Full-frontal Frida Kahlo. On August 15, I'll call your name over and over and over until grackles descend upon my shoulders, shrouding my eyes with stygian wings. I'll collect those feathers for fans, fluttering these in parades on *tu día de fiesta*. In the end, you'll welcome me as death's daughter, Milady of the Shadows. Meanwhile, I pay tribute, my fists filled with miniature icons, melted wax, molten magma, the moan of a mystical *derecho*, a sword lily, and a clutch of shiny, obsidian feathers.

Clouds shrouded dusk,
gracing me, I felt,
with your gelid shadow

*Las nubes envolvieron el crepúsculo*
*honrándome, sentí,*
*con tu sombra gélida*

# Our Lady of the Holiest Death: Santissima Muerte

Not canonized, Saint Death was homeless before being adopted by the under-class. When she realized she could provoke dreams, *Santissima Muerte* hailed her fans, held an Open House. A meet-and-greet with the narco-lord, *la puta*, the criminal, the rebel — but no selfies, though pure of bone, charcoal eyed, and naturally slim. After she vowed neutral morality, artists began to ink her likeness on arms or legs. Devotees nibble tiny chocolate skulls on her feast day, hoping mortality can be as sweet. Like a crafty real estate agent, The Bony Lady has already selected that final resting place, the closing date. A sinister guardian, each day she slips into your shadow. Quietly patient. Hanging overhead like a mute wind chime.

> Saint Death needs no gifts
> empty-handed, you're welcomed
> shake hands with omnipotence and helplessness

> *Santa Muerte no necesita regalos*
> *con las manos vacías, eres bienvenido*
> *estrechar la mano con omnipotencia y desamparo*

# Poltergeists on President Street

The memory knocks insistently, rattles its chain. The story retold, summoned, shared like leftovers from a phantom feast. My uncle's voice, an incantation that wiped the table clean of holiday food, poured the chill down the backs of our collars, goosefleshed our arms, as he explained how most ghosts are a disappearing act, but poltergeists engineer noisy return engagements. Vaudevillians of the void, greedy for a live audience.

A lifetime ago, his weekly poker game was dinner-theatre for restless spirits stuck in a haunted house. He carried in his gut hunger boxed inside the Great Depression, festering impatience, unquiet cravings. Nicotine nursed him daily, except when he donned altar-boy drag: cassock and surplice. The priest would elevate the host to an invisible God, his thurible filling the air with holy smoke. "Saints have no opportunity to stay dead," he thought, cupping a fist to the flame, inhaling an unfiltered Lucky Strike behind the rectory as his eyes scanned his surroundings and a "Room for Rent" drifted into view.

Complaints had carved an abyss between himself and his parents. They were inhospitable to the stink of stogies and cigarettes that fueled rounds of poker, angling their eyes like a crucified Christ, imploring the card players to quit. He needed a new venue, and offering rent money was his ace.

He ran enthusiastically up the stoop as a wan housewife ghosted into view, her face wreathed by a French inhale. A deal was struck for two games during weeknights, eight in a month, paid in advance. From an inner sanctum, a room he could not see, an unearthly falsetto shrieked, dimming the sunshine, roaring into his ears. "We have ghosts," she explained. "No extra charge."

Now those long-ago scares rose like steam, in the same way a flayed turkey breast releases its heat to the carving knife. Then came not the rapping, tapping Poe heard on his chamber door but the crashing, smashing of crockery shelved in china cabinets, glassware thrown at the stove, forcing the players to their feet, hunting for the source of the commotion, only to find nothing. To my uncle's eye, though, there were no cabinets — at least, not anymore. There had been, at one time, but the furious being continued smashing them, in their absence, decades later.

On other evenings, spooks would overturn the table, sending hearts and clubs airborne, alarming all. Haunting memories must have gnawed at the apparition's loneliness, continuing a ferocious domestic drama, echoing long ago chaos.

Priests came and went, their blessings, novenas, incense, prayers brittle as glass. Nothing lived in these invocations: no exorcism, no catharsis.

Collectively, our blood forgets to surge and flow as we shiver on the brink of climax. My uncle's closing act, ventriloquy, fills the room with unhinged cackling, a poltergeist maniacally gleeful. Proud of its performance as our soup pot boils dry and our percolator shrieks.

Years after, I dream of what must have happened to wind a spirit so angrily to that house: a slow-cooked rage, the soughing wind taunting the drawn shades, tattered scullery wallpaper scuffed by body slams. A furious spouse. Abuse accumulated, stoking a fire in the belly. Well-oiled revenge readying, seething, sharpening a six-inch boning knife. A marital ragout splattered across the wall. Now a dirge lullabies her ears as she swoons around the house, searching for a shovel, lozenging the word burial under her tongue. She begins her maniacal laughter.

Tomorrow's empty jar of morning fills with men in white coats and a restraining garment nearly split open by wild whoops of merriment, freedom from her husband's rage. At last there's a sense of the future humming.

Except it would not end there. Emotions drowned in this bloody kitchen would resurface, be regurgitated. Have the last laugh.

# An Ideal Lost in Night-Mists

**Blood's Kiss** — November 2nd  nightfall

I learned to be immortal from blood's kiss.
He taught me how to be a ghost part-time.

Like trees, we've bound ourselves below without
Burial, cocooned in soil, still sentient,
Possessed of appetites, required to feast.

Count D.'s companion now, all time dissolves.

Acquainted with the night, ageless, preserved,
We visit after dusk for sustenance.

My roommate Megan looks surprised. I smile.
Her armature is shifting. She's obsessed
With curiosity — the how and why.

First we embrace. She's glad to see I'm safe,
While mentioning police, strange questioning,
Their sketch created for the poster.  "Here,"
Says Megan. "Take a look."  I move in close,
Bestow my greatest gift: eternity.

***

**Missing, Classified as Undead** — November 2nd  afternoon

    Hallowe'en decorations still dotted their dorm, achingly orange, when detectives filed in, rust running off the hinges like fresh blood. Handmade missing posters, plastered with the police sketch, fueled the hums that won't quiet, unplugged from the lyrics sung to welcome discovery.
    Present for their Q-and-A: Megan, a roommate paired via lottery, neither confidante nor co-conspirator. She who was absent — Annabelle — left no trace. According to biblical interpretations, no harbingers of menace had loomed: ad-

dictions, failing grades, anorexia, bizarre online screeds. Evidence cleaved no flesh from bone: her purse placid on a pillow, no signs of forced entry, no signs of a struggle with a bogeyman lured by heat.

Their dorm room now a photographed crime scene, tension divides Megan's mind in a desperate rush and roil. Who? A guy they trusted? A clever serial killer who'd return to claim Megan next?

Investigators prod her to travel backwards, like storytellers, recounting the last time Annabelle was heard from. They scrutinize the wall calendar, Nov. 1st, All Saints Day, its childish scrawl: "Count D. / Volodya / Vova — 8 PM meet-up" and a crumpled, discarded October page peppered with male names like buckshot, the detritus of dating apps.

Cooperation is truth enveloped by a stringent sun. But facts forget the night harbors its own dialect. Words withhold her odd dream — surely that's all it was. Ushered in by a malodorous air of ancient dirt and gravecloths, a shape-shifting bat flew in, its enormous wingspan not unlike a black satin cloak. Megan squirreled under blankets, the room blotting to utter darkness. "When my alarm clock rang, I saw my roommate was gone," is all she'll tell investigators. They leave.

Alone now, in bed, on edge, Megan hears a loose floorboard creak, notices Annabelle's closet door ajar, as if something's slipping through the in-between, staking virgin space as if this was an outpost of an empire about to be invaded. Megan floods the room with the harsh institutional fluorescent fixture they've rarely used. Rifling through empty shoeboxes, she spies a diary whose locked flap yields to scissors, unbound by promises. Print-outs from chats shiver her full awake, compel her to read these artifacts, fascinating as a mummy's tape unraveling.

Count D: Do you believe in fate? In an *ideal lost in night-mists?*
Lady A: Kewl.
Count D: Child, you are salting my wounds with capricious teasing.
Lady A: Tell me yr name irl — the one behind yr screen name: Count D.

The stench of mildewed autumn leaves makes her look around. Annabelle is watching her.

***

**Dating the Undead** — October 29th   evening

His dating profile states he's a Virgo with Scorpio rising. He owns a castle, digs "blood diamonds," and he's 7,398 kms away from me.

First off he asks about my bloodtype, if I've ever been anemic, if I sleep with my dorm window open, and if I consider myself to be an adventuress.

I message him back, coyly requesting pics … inside this castle. I ask: do u really live in Transylvania a.k.a. Romania? If so, how would we meet up irl?

He replies I must never worry — he can be at my doorstep in a flash.

Sure. Ha-ha, I type, playing along. Send pics of u with yr castle, I repeat.

Instead he sends pics of his jewelry vault and apologizes that his selfies rarely come out right. He explains that the thing about modern photography is that it's been stunted by the cowardice of credulity. He adds an smh.

Obviously, he's seen many profile pics doctored with PhotoShop or massaged with beauty filters. I'm about to check which pics I uploaded this week. Instead I Google Transylvania — Wow! Snow-capped peaks! — and ask if he skis or hikes.

He replies his castle is near the Carpathians but forces of destiny conspired to make him fonder of flying than bipedalism, none of which diminishes his enthusiasm for athletic ingenues.

A new pic pops up — a black and white sketch, all smoky charcoal — his dark eyes deeper than the diving pool on campus. Even from here they manage to pierce my composure. His clothing is out-dated though elegant — from a high-end vintage shop. Like the ones in SoHo.

As if he's reading my mind — *but how could he?* — he admits to being "an old soul, a connoisseur, a poet manqué." Collecting leather-bound autographed volumes of poetry, he adds, is a consummate delight.

Expecting he'll ask about my faves, I'm recalling which poets I've read in class. Instead he sends me an autographed flyleaf signed Mihai Eminescu, a name I've never seen on the gram.

Then he posts a poem. Probably it's better in the original than what Google translates. Still the first four lines are sweetly romantic and I send them back in English:

> *Oh, ideal lost in night-mists of a vanished universe:*
> *People who would think in legends — all a world who spoke in verse;*
> *I can see and think and hear you — youthful scout which gently nods*
> *From a sky with different starlights, other Edens, other gods.*

He asks: Do you believe in fate? In an *"ideal lost in night-mists"*?

I text back "kewl."

He replies that I am salting his wounds with capricious teasing. OMG, I think. He *is* a poet. Now I want to know his name irl — instead of his screen name: *Count D*. Honestly, that D made me wonder if it's a new code for "expect dick pics." But he's not a creep. Sure is different tho. And while he's typing, I Google "Virgo with Scorpio rising" and one post says this: "A Virgo Sun Scorpio Rising definitely wants an obsessive love where they will be hooked on the object of their desire." *Obsessive love!* Bussin'.

His name irl bubbles up on my screen: Volodya. WTF?

Then he adds his Mom calls him Vova and do I like his nickname?

"Lit!" I reply.

He keeps texting faster now — at an unnatural pace. Almost like he's telepathing instead of typing. Weird but flattering. Not like the cut-n-paste crap some guys send to every chick. We flirt. He's seductive but never nasty. Kinda thrilling in an eerie way. I imagine his long, slender fingers removing those gaudy rings and caressing my face. I blush and I'm relieved he can't see me — until he asks why I'm flushed. Do I have fever? Am I fully vaxxed?

Before I can reply, he types a question: Do u have plans for Samhain?

I admit I do — but just with friends who have an annual picnic on Hallowe'en on their roof deck. It overlooks Sixth Avenue, so we can watch New York City's costume parade.

There's a long pause. I wonder if his WiFi disconnected up there in the Carpathian Mountains — or wherever he's texting from.

Then he's back. The 30th is his special number cos he was born on the 30th of August, he tells me. It would mean a great deal if we could meet up tomorrow — on October 30th.

Again I have plans, which is the point of dating apps, am-i-right? But we're super vibing. I don't wanna be a downer so I ask: Nov. 1st? It's crazy but suddenly I feel a jolt through my cell, a surreal tingle through my veins.

He texts, YESSSSSS!!! — the hiss of all caps sibilants already running down my spine.

I tease back — cos no way do I believe it — r u gonna send me a plane tix?

Faster than lightspeed, he replies his chauffeur will collect me in NYC on Nov. 1st — about 8-ish.

I text that's awesome. *Collect* impresses me. But also brings to mind a butterfly collection: beautiful creatures pinned down. I brush away my silly thought to read his next text.

Rodomontade is odious, he texts, but forgive my humble-brag. Crypto has been good to me and afforded me the luxury of acquiring a Rolls Royce from India, a model called "New Ghost." I am fond of crypt — fond of *crypto trading*. Opportunities 24/7. Enough gasconade, my sweet. *Pana atunci, dragamea*!

Really working Google translate tonight. His words meant: "Until then, my dearest." Guess he has a dreamy foreign accent and that's why his English is . . . unusual. Before I can reply, he texts 3 heart emojis. I ask if there's a dress code — but it seems he's left me on read cos just dead space follows.

My dorm mate Megan hung a wall calendar with moon phases and holidays. Flipping up the page to see if there's a full moon on the first of November, I notice it's the Catholic holyday Feast of All Saints. The day of the dead.

***

Note: excerpt from "Venus and Madonna" by Romanian poet Mihai Eminescu [1850 — 1889].

# Haunting

# Abecedarian: Apparitions Beckon Cautiously, Determined

Apparently, apparitions can see clearly in daylight. They spied me
butterflied on the dusty tiled floor of the top floor's bathroom.
Cautiously, I'd hidden after the haunted house tour, cupping lullaby silk in my palms,
determined to wander alone through this mysterious mansion, quietly
exploring each room alone, weighing my plans, high off uninhibitedness,
forensic equipment squirreled in my backpack,
gravel boned ghost hunting gadgetry such as Geiger counters and
high-tech electro magnet field (EMF) detectors.
Invisible presences must be made interesting to YouTube viewers even if it's
just cheap window-dressing: clicking, ticking, flashing lights.
Kinetics, the effect of forces, bait an audience to keep watching and subscribing.
Less scientific methods are often used, too, to sharpen showmanship.
Money? Though meaningful, that's the lowest priority. I am an old-fashioned
necromancer, a ghost whisperer, on a personal mission,
outlier and insider both, my ideas replenished by every risk that scaffolds them.
Pseudoscience attracts followers, funds junkets like this visit — to a phantom's lair.
Questions become easier to answer, melt in my mouth when the camera is on me.
Reanimated now, pixelated poreless spirits pulse with curiosity, rather too
shady to be relatable to humans, but I'm ready for this and
telepath my plans to the group, presences of absentees, sentient beings
undone by mortality. They demonstrate their approval by manifesting more fully.
Vitreous before, anticipation has coaxed them into clearer visibility.
*When?* They telepath back to me. Like a sorceress, I produce my wand.
X-level excitement smudges their forms huddled near heavy drapery.
Yesteryear's chains lighten and detach. *Now? All of us?* Palpable is their
zeal as I thread each one backwards through time's needle — and release them.

# Don't Monetize Those Poltergeists

Don't try to monetize a poltergeist.
Greed's bad ghost karma can't be rectified.

Disgraced, divorced, and homeless, one man saw
Redemption's out-stretched hand where others paused.
Abandoned, curiously cheap to rent,
This mansion's past inspired its second chance.

Accomplices were needed. Two arrived
When Gerald Laughlin hatched his hapless plot
To profit from aged, angry entities.

In 1967, he lured folks
Who paid to tour dark rooms suffused with gloom
Inhabited by visible deceased
Who followed paying guests — but would not speak.

Published accounts have chronicled his woes.
Too many harrowing encounters there
Encouraged Gerald and his cohorts — men
Who never were right-minded after that —
To flee, unseen foes hanging on their coats.

Since bad ghost karma can't be overcome,
Investigate who's haunting your house first.
Respect the dead, whose turmoil can't be priced.
Don't try to monetize sly poltergeists.

\*\*\*

Note: After a professional crisis cratered his chiropractic career and his marriage, Dr. Gerald Alexander Laughlin [c. 1926 — 24 Jun 2001] needed inexpensive lodgings and a new purpose. A dilapidated 33-room mansion [1161 N. Liberty at Atlantic Ave.], rumored to house inhospitable spirits, was vacant and well below market value. In 1967, Laughlin transformed the 19th century residence into New Castle, Pennsylvania's first "commercial" haunted house. Mayhem and death ensued. Afterwards, a mysterious fire consumed the vacant mansion.

# Abecedarian: Honeymoon Homicide, 129 Spring Street, 1799

All arsy varsey I went over him, our new boarder. But a wretched
beard splitter and scoundrel he turned out to be, sweet words stealing my
chastity, giving me a belly. "I shant give caudel without tying the knot!"
Distressed I was, in this condition, when he proposed, slipped on a ring.
Elopement. How romantic. December 22, 1799 would be a day I'd not
forget, leaving my family's abode to start married life with my handsome
groom, Levi Weeks, a man of parts. Suddenly he spoke roughly, as if I were a
harlot or hoyden. This was uncharacteristic of my gentle lover, who became
impatient when new boots slowed my pace. One moment my
jemmy fellow, then ill-tempered, and strangely out of
kelter when I said, "The chapel's off Vesey Street. Why are we walking towards
Lispenard's Meadow instead?" His response was to give me a basting.
"Murder! Murder! Oh, save me!" I screamed. He laughed. "Thought I was a
ninny who could be trapped by a bastard child?" His hands squeezed the breath
out of me, dumped me into a well. At his trial, Uncle Elias Ring testified that he was
"pale and much agitated" when he returned to Greenwich Street alone. After Levi was ac-
quitted, Cousin Hope Sands hexed his lawyer Alexander Hamilton, a curse that stuck.
Rage honed my supernatural prowess, taught me how to wreak havoc on men.
Stumbling into my sphere, a tipsy woman is gowned, bejeweled, and masked.
The well, my wretched wet grave, is now part of the basement in a victualling house.
Usually, only gaunt nippers, dressed in black, and carrying silver trays
ventured downstairs. Bored, I've occasionally locked them up in the dark
wine cellar. A burly drunken sot is following her, disheveled hair in greasy,
xanthic waves. She's alarmed. With intention, I aim a jereboam to smash his skull.
Yowling in fright at his blood puddle, the lady lifts her skirts and runs upstairs. Properly
zocked, the souse lays at my feet blank-eyed. Zounds, this calls for a champagne toast.

***

Note: Rumored to be pregnant, Gulielma Elmore Sands, age 22, was last seen alive on December
22, 1799 when she left with Levi Weeks. Her body was found on January 2, 1800 in the Manhattan
Well in Lispenard's Meadow, then the northern boundary of New York City.

**Lexicon of 18th century terms:**

arsy varsey — head over heels
beard splitter — a man much given to wenching
give caudel — to give birth
jemmy fellow — a smart, spruced up gentleman
out of kelter — out of sorts, in poor spirits
basting — a beating
victualling house — commercial establishment where food and beverages are served; tavern
nippers — young errand boys
xanthic — a yellowish color
zock — to strike a hard blow, to sock a person with force

# Hallowe'en Window Painting

Ghosts rise, my brush broad-stroking outdoor glass,
The store already closed, fluorescents on,
Illuminating my half-finished sketch.

Stray skeletons, masked witches, pumpkin kings,
All smiles and hope, parade down bat streaked blocks,
Embracing trick-or-treat bags — pirate's loot.

Despite my weariness, my brush takes flight,
Creating doors that open to a reign
Of orange bliss just harvested: plump yams,
Carrots, spaghetti squash. A scarecrow smirks,
His jack-o-lantern head lit, menacing
Owls, bellowing harsh candlelight. Unnerved,
I freeze, aware I'm not alone, about
To curse the closed mouth sky, providing no
Clues where this strange farm lies — nor how to leave.

Sly skeletons, loud witches, pumpkin kings
Approach, aggressive country primitives.

My horsehair brush is weaponized, collects
Enough white tempera to cover each one,
Obliterating malefactors with
Ruthless efficiency. Strong stubborn winds
Convey me to a secret corridor
That's underneath the Brooklyn store where I
Was working on my mini masterpiece —
*Completed* in my absence. Can it be?

A painted scarecrow meets my eyes and winks.

# A Lighter
# Shade

TS I MUST NOT FRIGHTEN THE PETS I MU
TS I MUST NOT FRIGHTEN THE PETS
S I MUST NOT FRIGHTEN THE PETS
TS I MUST NOT FRIGHTEN THE PETS
TS I MUS NOT FRIGHTEN THE P
TS I M T FRIGHTEN THE
TS I N NOT FRIGHTEN THE

# Emily Post's "Etiquette Book for Ghosts"

Emily Post's *Etiquette Book for Ghosts*
Is a must since spirits are unruly,
Annoying, crass, and insistent — truly.
Tactless phantoms offended?  Just quote Post!

Are spooks invasive, when they might have phoned?
This rule book helps avoid unpleasantries.
Emily Post's *Etiquette Book for Ghosts* —
It's a must when spirits get unruly.

It's your nature to be a gracious host.
But poltergeists will taunt guests unduly.
Spectres will scare domestic pets mutely.
Next time wraiths visit, be prepared to quote
Emily Post's *Etiquette Book for Ghosts*.

My copy's autographed. Excuse my boast.

# The Widow's Missing Necklace, October 1977

He promised everything, in time, improves.
If wedlock's root is trust, is love removed
By death? His widow finds it hard to sleep
Alone. Bereavement's hollowed her pale cheeks,
Uncaressed. Robbed of joy, her spirit's bruised.

An anniversary gift, precious jewels,
Cannot be found. This necklace was not moved
Nor worn since he fell ill. Again she weeps.
       He promised everything.

Ghost husband, undetected, jangled loose
Her precious pearls, its faulty catch fine-tuned.
Repairing jewelry does not come cheap —
Despite the fact this goldsmith was deceased.
He buried it in bedding, feeling shrewd.
My aunt thinks spooks exist. This can't be proved.
       He promised everything.

\*\*\*

Note: My Uncle Larry returned to his widow's bedroom — to drop off the repaired 25th silver anniversary necklace — in late October 1977. His funeral had taken place twelve months prior.

# Babysitting a Bone in Washington Square Park, Once a Potter's Field

The bone kept singing. Long grass and scrub disguised it, half-asleep in lime-white dusk, like an earthworm displaced to a sun-warmed walkway. Flesh once enveloped every tender curve. Lungs once expanded, bellow-like, rehearsing an anthem. This tune, neither melodious nor doomed, needed a more generous interpretation than I could manage, while petting it with the side of my shoe. Pleased to meet you, Femur. Death flattens a corpse's understory, its ancestry a forgotten dialect, but long bones persevere. Once a potter's field agitated this soil, 20,000 deceased, indigent New Yorkers were shoveled over, poverty the public's natural blindfold. Transformed into Washington Square Park, a silhouette of rooftops fringed four sides. Femur continued crooning, huffing at dandelions, angling for one monumental moment. Carefully nudged under a park bench, garbage bags camping around us, Femur hummed when stroked by my toes. Watching the trees turn black, watching uniformed police locking the gates, watching buildings bleed together, the sole of my foot warmed the bare bone until blue suits ambled over to start their questioning. Disinterested in this century's utterances, the bone continued singing, moonstruck as earth's last gasp.

\*\*\*

Note: From 1797 — 1825, what is now Washington Square Park was the City's Potter's Field, where thousands of people, including the unidentified, the indigent, and those who died of yellow fever, were buried.

# Hulda, the Westchester Witch

Hulda the healer, well known far and wide,
Resided in a cottage by Spook Rock,
Mistrusted by her neighbors who denied
Her remedies cured illnesses. They mocked

All foreigners whose accents or lifestyles
Were different. Unmarried, fearless, plain,
Bohemia trained, Hulda was reviled,
Called "witch" despite good deeds, which were disdained,

Arcane procedures thought to be witchcraft.
During combat with British soldiers, she
Was slain. Townspeople hearing she had passed,
Retrieved her corpse, conveyed her home, agreed

To bury Hulda decently. Surprised
Were they, discovering a Bible there
With medical books. She had been baptized.
A sage deserved respect. For years, they erred.

Famed authors season stories with her spice,
Attracting tourists to her tomb, enticed
To learn about this worthy — once despised.
Her ghost protects townsfolk from poltergeists,
Observing from Spook Rock on moonless nights.

\*\*\*

Note: A headstone for Hulda, crafted in the style of an 18th-century monument with a winged soul soaring above her name, was erected at the Old Dutch Church burial ground in Sleepy Hollow, remembering "Hulda of Bohemia" who "died c. 1777. Herbalist, Healer, Patriot. Felled by British while protecting the Militia. Buried here in gratitude for her sacrifice."

# Acknowledgments

Samhain
> — in *SFPA Hallowe'en Poetry Reading*, October 2021

A Sleepy Hollow Hallowe'en
> — in Zoetic Press's *NonBinary Review*, Issue 27, Shared Worlds, Spring 2022; rpt in *Litmora Literary Magazine*, Issue SPOOK!, October 29, 2023

Dracula Plans His Hallowe'en Soiree
> — in *Bewildering Stories*, Issue 1019, October 27, 2023, rpt in *The Raven Review*, Fall 2023 issue; rpt in *Tales from the Moonlit Path*, Hallowe'en 2023; rpt in *Penumbra,* Hallowe'en 2023

Hallowe'en Horror,  October 31, 2005
> — in *Quail Bell,* January 12, 2023

Bell, Book, and Candle
> — in *Granfalloon*, Fall 2022; rpt in *Sirens Call Ezine*, Issue 63, October 25, 2023

Secrets of the Spell
> — in *Granfalloon*, Winter 2021; rpt in *Dreich Magazine* 2, Season 4, February 2022; rpt in *Bewildering Stories*, Issue 943, March 2022

Spellcasting on Samhain
> — in *Wine Cellar Press*, Issue: The Veil Between the Worlds, February 4, 2023; rpt in *Bewildering Stories*, Issue 988,  March 4, 2023

A Night on Bald Mountain, All Hallows' Eve
> — in *HallowZine*, Issue 2, October 31, 2021

Elizabeth Siddal Rossetti, Cemetery Superstar
— in *Spectral Realms*, Issue 17, April 2022

Erasure at Nightfall
— in *Coffin Bell Journal*, May 2022; rpt in *Blood Moon Rising*, Issue 90, January 16, 2023

The Hallowe'en Homicides on October 31, 1981
— in *Quail Bell*, January 12, 2023

Our Lady Of Holy Death I
— in *West Trade Review*, Spring 2022

Our Lady Of Holy Death II
— in *Sirens Call Ezine*, Issue 60, Hallowe'en 2022

Poltergeists on President Street
— in *Spectral Realms*, Issue 16, Jan. 2022; revised for *The Other Folk*, June 16, 2022

Blood's Kiss
— in *Star\*Line*, Issue 45.4, October 4, 2022

An Ideal Lost in Night-Mists
— in *Querencia Press*, Autumn Anthology, October 2022

Abecedarian: Apparitions Beckon Cautiously, Determined
— in *Abyss and Apex*, Summer issue, 2022

Don't Try to Monetize a Poltergeist
— in *Timber Ghost Press*, March 14, 2023

Hallowe'en Window Painting
— in *Bewildering Stories*, Issue 987, February 26, 2023; rpt *Sirens Call Ezine*, Issue 63, Hallowe'en 2023; rpt in *Litmora Literary Magazine*, Issue SPOOK!, October 29, 2023

Emily Post's "Etiquette Book for Ghosts"
        — in *Bewildering Stories*, Issue 911, July 2021

The Widow's Missing Necklace, October 1977
        — in *BFS Horizons*, Issue # 14, September 2022

Baby-Sitting a Bone in Washington Square Park, Once a Potter's Field
        — in *Abyss and Apex*, Winter issue, January 1, 2022

# About LindaAnn LoSchiavo

A native New Yorker, Elgin Award winner LindaAnn LoSchiavo is a member of the British Fantasy Society, Horror Writers Association, the Science Fiction Poetry Association, and the Dramatists Guild of America.

Her writing has received multiple nominations for the Pushcart Prize, Best of the Net, Firecracker Award, Balcones Poetry Prize, Paterson Poetry Prize, Quill and Ink, Elgin Award, Rhysling Award, and an IPPY.

Current books: "Messengers of the Macabre," "Vampire Ventures," and "Always Haunted: Hallowe'en Poems," "Apprenticed to the Night," and "Felones de Se: Poems about Suicide."

Twitter: @Mae_Westside
YouTube: LindaAnn Literary:
https://www.youtube.com/channel/UCHm1NZIlTZybLTFA44wwdfg

Wild Ink Publishing is new to the publishing industry, which means we are able to showcase some of the brightest wordsmiths by unleashing the shackles that usually stop people from publishing traditionally.

wild-ink-publishing.com

Printed in the USA
CPSIA information can be obtained
at www.ICGtesting.com
CBHW081158090924
14064CB00010B/167

9 781958 531730